A Good Broom

A Good Broom

Poems

Regina O'Melveny

Sheila-Na-Gig Editions

Cover art: Regina O'Melveny, *Broom*, watercolor
Author Photo: Bill O'Melveny

ISBN: 978-1-962405-90-4
Library of Congress Control Number: 2026934391

Sheila-Na-Gig Editions
Russell, KY
Hayley Mitchell Haugen, Editor
www.sheilanagigblog.com

Acknowledgments

I'm grateful to the editors of the following periodicals in which some of these poems first appeared:

Cider Press Review: "A/wake"

Dos Gatos Press: "End of February"

Last Stanza: "Timeout" (formerly "Toward")

Nature Writing: "Birds Across the Moon," "Sea Plowed by Dolphins"

Red Wheelbarrow: "Mountain" Second Prize

San Diego Poetry Annual Anthology: "Homage to a Snakefly" Honorable Mention Steve Kowit Poetry Prize

Today Marymount College: "Deer"

For Bill, Adrienne, Danny, Kaela, Charlie
& all our wild kin

Contents

Hot Winds, Wildfire, Ochre Leaves

Long Shadows, Rain, Quickening Roots

Ask the questions that have no answers.
. . . Plant sequoias.
Say that your main crop is the forest
that you did not plant, that you will not live to harvest.

—Wendell Berry

Strong Winds, Sudden Bloom

Why I Write

to mend a torn fabric
follow a loose strand of words through ancient forests of memory

dream with eyes open
witness the everyday gift

dance with bees in their golden chambers
play with infinity, humbly

sing the morning, hum afternoon, hold silence
under my tongue at night

embrace the sheltering trees of childhood
hold my grandfather's hand, taste my grandmother's lemon meringue

love again,
burn rage to ash and ink

breathe beauty and comb the hair of the muses
braid my granddaughter's tangles

kiss the slick frog at the wishing well
welcome the stranger

smell vanilla and chocolate
touch the warp and weft of the mind's constant loom

pray for the wind that clears grey thickets from the heart
listen for questions that have no answers.

Bare Branches of March

Tonight
the moon falls
into the well
at the bottom of
the dream.
I never hoped
for such joy
but it comes anyway.
Spring awakens
everything
in dark water,
roots white as night-
planets shining.
Even the body.

Come Spring,
Even the Woman With Grey Braids Will Dance

The winter-stark trees I view from the plane's oval
pane on descent toward Corcaigh Ireland
blur to pale green on ascent a week later.

A red-tipped green that must be the color
Hildegard of Bingen called *soul* or the color sweet
stuttering words must be, slipping from a young girl's lips

the first time she ever tastes love, or
the quick color of everything hidden for months,
even years, that greens in bright bursts of faith.

How else can I answer the season, other than
ache for the life I didn't know possible,
my ribs growing supple as shoots with each breath

breaking into blossom and leaf, my old heart
swelling again as if I'm that maiden holding hands
with the wind, spilling flowers from her tongue?

Peach Trees

I cut a branch from the peach tree
outside my window, tight buds
curled like pink baby fists
in sleep, beginning to open.
Every spring I welcome these sweet
nubs of joy against leaden gloom.
My friend Gordon, gone many years,
once gave me an old wood assemblage
with shutter baffles pink as
the bloom out the window.

He'd lived with the Diné who called him
Blankets Thrown Down on the Ground,
his rumpled clothes
always covered with paint.
Their hogans were round.
They couldn't understand how
we live in houses with corners
where troubled spirits might dwell
waving their arms like scorched trees,
bleeding sap.

When Kit Carson rounded up all
the Diné hiding in Canyon de Chelly,
he ordered his men to set fire
to their orchards, hundreds
of budding peach trees like young girls
swaying deep in the canyon, pride
of the tribe, torched. What kind
of man would do such a thing?
asks a Diné grandmother,
weaving red and black on her loom.

All year Gordon's assemblage echoes
the pink where my peach tree
gathers herself into bloom
at the corner where I pray.

Pray for all the ghost trees,
limbs flung up in smoke, ash,
charred roots mourning the people.
Unspoken burdens. What kind
of man? a Diné grandmother asks.
I ask, what kind of people?

The same kind who could
order the Diné to walk
The Long Walk, hundreds
of miles, thousands
dying of hunger along the dry road
of exile from their land.
Carson spoke their language,
promised he'd take
care of them, lured them away
from the canyon.

Some people where I live
drive lead nails into longstanding trees
to kill them. They're blocking
the view! They holler
at city council, though they already
claim broad views.
They'll always profit from more.
Some will pay hatchet-men
to cut down neighbors' trees
when no one is home.

What is my prayer now?
May we pry hammers, chainsaws
and matches away from clenched hearts.
May trees grow in our words.
May we be restored by the flowering branch.
May views open up in the dense shade
of our minds, and though bereft of trees,
may we plant more
in this blackened soil
that lies speechless between us.

April

> Bind grasses to build a hut and don't give up . . .
> Turn the light to shine within and return.
>
> —Old man Shitou

Every day we return.
The hut we built
sprouts weeds
falls in on one side.

The apple we left there
turns brown from
fine teeth marks—
a hungry mouse.

Even mushrooms grow here.
Ants link up
a living path from one
corner to another.

No hermit is ever alone.
Turn the light within.
No end to darkness,
no end to our multitude.

Bind grasses and
don't give up.
How fragrant they are!
Spring hums in the blades.

A Good Broom

Every morning
I sweep the wooden
deck by the pond.
Every season distinct.
Every day.
Moment.
The same.

Today I wear a large hat
and bump my head
hard on a low limb
as I sweep leaves
and tiny avocados
that for some reason
didn't set on the tree.

Yet it yielded more
this year than ever.
Maybe thanks
to beehives
I set up last fall
or the oddly
warm winter.

Squirrels love even
the smallest fruits.
Sometimes I sweep up
their nests,
twigs intertwined
with stuffing plucked
from our cushions.

The wind returns
what was stolen
though I don't mind.

The squirrels may have
all the fluff they want, a gift
for their flamboyant
feats in the trees.

I also consider a gift
the branch that whacked
my head, made me stop,
hold one hand
on the stinging bonk,
one hand on top
of my worthy broom.

Though I mean
to trim that branch,
instead
I bend lower
and sweep.
From now on
I'll bow to the tree.

Springtails

When I step out the back door to welcome the rain, I'm stopped
by a puddle seething with violet specks on the stairs.

What's this? My skin crawls a little. Myriad creatures
the size and shape of lavender buds clump together

while outliers on the bowed surface pop
like crazy florets or wild seeds springing open.

I watch them a long time. What are they doing,
mating or defending rank in the puddle?

Clustering for protection, announcing spring,
or like me celebrating long awaited rain?

No reason joy can't be universal. After all I hear
the trees in their deep roots thrum, in their leaves exult.

I catch the glad scent thrown by pungent wild sage. Feel
drought recede, a bad memory that no longer shrivels the heart.

May we too, in our small puddle, let go dry fears and fling
ourselves toward the unknown with all the marvelous pluck
of the small.

Mountain

> And no hurt or harm be done
> Anywhere along the holy mountain.
> —John O'Donohue, from *Benedictus*

Here in my garden, small mountain
of fresh earth kicked up
in holy dig by gophers

who sink my artichokes,
whole plants shaken, toppled,
vanished, unintended offerings.

Here the anthill, fine crater mount
entry to the underworld
immaculate community

each one working for all
all for one queen at center
who oviposits life after life.

Here the far mountain in dream
after a friend's estrangement,
a twisted road, difficult journey.

I want to bless, release,
but the road writhes,
steepens, stops.

Here the mountain where I live
scrabbled by spring wind
that tosses branches,

moans all the way
from pungent desert
and bears in its wake

not calm but a blue edge
or uneasy bellwether.
I lose words, trust,

and must come back to
the rugged mountains
that offer no pass

until I see that the holy
montane reach
is the whole of things

that must be circled,
walked, ascended,
descended over and over

received in silence,
venerated, smelt, tasted,
seen every day.

I hold it, mountain in hand
and pray, let no harm come
to gopher, ant, or friend.

Homage to a Snakefly

The little boy points out
a tiny creature snug in the seam between
my daughter's white kitchen wall and ceiling.
At first I think—a termite?
But no. An unknown thing,
a dark speck has come to visit.
Up on a ladder I coax her into a jar
then we watch her magnified,
winged dragon if dragons grew
half an inch long, as she slinkily stretches
her elegant neck to observe us in return.
What is fat fing? my two-year-old grandson asks.
I look up the little dragon
and find it's called a snakefly.
The long needle stinger that wows us
is really an ovipositor, handy for
slipping eggs under tree-bark.
When larval, a snakefly can scurry
both forwards and amazingly backwards
across the mulchy forest floor.
Across blue millennia.
A living fossil, her kind once roamed
Mesozoic jungles when
Africa and South America
hadn't yet rifted apart.
We humans nowhere to be seen.
What does she impart?
The wondrous nature of our kin.
The boundless power of the small.
The invisible and disregarded
world in all its delicate intimacy
creeping across the boundaries
of the human heart.
For here we are now, admiring her
then walking into the garden
we let the beautiful snakefly go.

Long Days, Cloud Decks Over the Ocean

What Am I Waiting For?

Maybe a celestial
hand that plunges
from the clouds,
touches my shoulder
to signify, you are good.
That old ache
for recognition
in all the wrong places.
Instead, here it is, simple
as a pebble at the edge
of a lake, June thaw.
The poem neither good
nor bad, intending some question,
some honesty. A small heft
in the palm.
The muse.
Even in her absence
I find my workable flaws.
What am I waiting for?
That may not be
the question after all,
but the place to which I return,
not desperation, but attention.
Then I can toss the pebble
into the water.

Rafting the Snake

Our guide says, *this river braids*
the waters, so it won't kick up rapids.
Though small granitic pebbles
spit and pop under our raft
like live things, quick memories
that bite the heart. Here we wind
between earthen dikes laid down
by glaciers tens of thousands of years ago.
Wild waters also course through my body.

Waters just melted from frozen lakes
where fish suspended, dreamt
slow dreams all winter
under ice so pure it's blue,
from mud so deep it's night, flowing.
The land is in me, even this watershed's
farthest source north in grizzly country,
glacial melt, the thousand rivulets come from fire,
steam, the hidden creeks of spring.

All come down to the river that combs
the land, layers stones and skulls,
whips back and forth through the valley,
carries us under keen white peaks that rise
blind seers at every turn, staunch mountains
that nonetheless shift, hone the blade-blue sky
and avalanche down in fierce love
for the river that takes up even the infinite
into its twisting glistening hands.

The Heft

As I read
under the maples
something swoops,
shunts wind
from its wings, settles
on the straw hat
I'm wearing.
The shadow
on the page before me—
a large bird
with a hooked beak.
No sound.
I'm motionless, stunned.
He dips his head,
looks and looks
but can't see me,
the warm post
beneath him.
Is god this light,
this heavy,
taloned?

For weeks since you
almost died,
I ponder faith or
my lack thereof.
Sit zazen,
light candles
to Saint Beatrice.
Even my father's spirit
comes from
the forest of death
to stand beside me.
I breathe slowly,
weighted with

the unknown.
When the hawk flies at last,
glides down the hill
below me,
I'm hollowed out
by awe.

Once the falcon-
headed man/
god of sky
and perpetual return,
Horus shone
with eyes of
sun and moon.
The blessing great.
Red-eyed,
black-capped
Cooper's hawk,
how can I
give thanks for
your heft?
Send the
small birds
of my poems
to your grasp,
their font hearts
beating amazed?

Or simply release,
as my father
once taught
when he passed
a red-tailed hawk
from his wrist to mine,
wings a muffled chant
as the hawk flew up
into an oak.

Then my father
was gone.
But you, my beloved
remain.
Spirit teaches silence,
brevity, attention.
Here, keen-eyed hawk,
this small offering.
Whenever you want
to rest on my head,
come. I'll hold still
beneath you.

the mountain is walking

every summer for
twenty-five years
we've gone to the mountain

to walk the great
granite flank
breathe the sky

swim in the mountain
lake beneath the fir and
pine clad peak

now the mountain
is walking
toward me

south
toward the large
city where I live

will I open
the door
will I open?

how can the mountain
fit in my home
how can it not be my guest?

here I say
to the mountain
sit I'll make tea

I'll make you the tea
of the five winds
I'll make you

the tea of silence
reverence
brevity

to my amazement
the mountain sits
the mountain rests

in my home and still
there is room for others
maybe a whole range

Timeout

In Buddhist sutras, *Ksana* is one seventy-fifth of a second. *Zazen*
on the quick. How can one keep up with this? Can't and yet. Snap
your fingers. Seventy-five *ksanas* flew by. Death that much closer.

The question tickles my mind as I lean into August
along the blue shore. The ocean stutters with wind.
Tangles of hoppers vex the edge of seawrack and ebb.

My body doesn't know the difference between. Here and there.
Sing: hit the road, Lack, and don'tcha come back no more,
no more, no more, no more. But the itch skitters back.

Oh yeah, a ball of gnats skips to the singsong sun.
Now the dog snaps at them and misses. Then he digs a hole to China
in the sand. Here. There. Everywhere. Nowhere. No more.

Time unzips kelpishly. The holdfast no longer. I walk.
I scratch my arm. That's it. A million *ksanas* gone.
Can you hear the cackling sea, the small guffaws of sandflies?

All I Can See

Not satisfied with views of the mountains, harbor,
and open sea, my uphill neighbors insist
on an unobstructed view, enabled by ordinance.
When asked what she wants, one neighbor says,
cut all the trees down, (over a hundred) *plant shrubs!*

Another neighbor, piano teacher chimes in,
the sound of chainsaws is music to my ears!
Already my friend's forty-year-old stone pines are down
and others cut to stubs. She paced her yard and wept.
They call it view restoration.

Those trees lent shade for my daughter and me walking
to school, gave us pungent relief in summer,
long contemplative shadows in winter.
In ancient Greece after enemies razed sacred groves,
the oracle warned *The more you eat the hungrier you will be!*

Today another neighbor lost palms and a great eucalyptus.
Chainsaws took three days to fell the trunk.
Limbs groaned, shook the earth as they plunged
in chunks, thuds I felt in my bones.
Great soul!

Once I lay sick on our couch, found solace
as I watched your branches sweep the sky in storm.
Now the sun's eye scorches gardens.
Everywhere the old gods are dying.
Even the new ones.

Kindness gone to grievance.
Neither sky nor trees are mine or yours.
The redbark eucalyptus stood rooted
in our midst with the resonance of a green prayer.
Now all I see is its ghost.

Third of An Acre

> They get to know that land,
> and they form a friendship with it.
>
> —Stan Rushworth

We've lived here for forty years.
Long enough to call
the coastal sage mountain, friend.
We're like other newcomers,
eucalyptus, jacarandas, cedars,
along with those who've set seed
and spread roots for hundreds of years,
wild cherry, dark toyon, sweet sagebrush.

Some were planted before
we arrived: desert senna,
coyote bush, coast redwoods.
Others I've brought home again:
willows and elderberry for birds,
ironwood, sumac, monkeyflower,
and all the wild wind-bright flowers:
poppies, tidy tips, lupines.

This is my happiest work.
Planting the old ones anew.
As I pat dirt around the young
sycamore, I see my grandparents'
sycamores, the dusty, spicy smell
that called to me, *come here child, cool off*
under our shade, play with our big fuzzy leaves,
the crisp hands of summer.

My garden also grew out
of mourning. Neighbors above us
exploited a law to increase broad
sea views, forced us to cut down

venerable old pines, eucalyptus,
spruce, ash and palms. Even
the red-barked eucalyptus
my daughter's wishing tree.

After walking among the ghost trees
a long time, I turned to the ancestors,
natives, oily pungent and sturdy,
and planted them where the dead
had opened up space and sun.
Planted wherever gaps appeared
when non-natives died—though I hold
nothing against them. I am one.

But now they need too much water.
Yet the global span of
this small garden heartens me.
Australian eucalyptus, European rosemary
African melaleuca, Asian hawthorn.
South American jacaranda.
I want to honor the whole array
even as the elders return.

To learn how the land bears
drought or deluge, heat, fog,
yields spring in January.
How the land, even more than this
third of an acre, claims me, calls on me
to heal the pungent balance
with a fierce pacific heart and wild green soul.
To call the land friend, to plant myself here.

Prayer Mountain

Dusk in August hangs
like a lantern about
to go out, snuffed by silence.
For a long moment none
of the shadowy angels that brood
hunched on branches
of the red fir, breathe.
This is the moment of
blue prayer gone grey,
gone stone, mute sap,
long thoughts that
touch the dark lip of night.
Some say angels never
close their eyes
but these begin to fall
asleep in chant where they forget
the burning gauze of day
unraveling.
Dreams come
with wind and forest rumor,
moss maidens rise from the lakes,
stones tell devotions, count
the centuries.
Lichens listen.
Even ants
in their underground halls
pause and nod to the mountain.

Visitations

I

I want to walk the mountains,
my pack spare, heart/mind wide open,
legs ready, body set for the high places
close to ancestor animals, trees and stones.
Where later, stars will bite like slivers
of beauty cast from the night sky.

Instead Queen Corona settles down
in my flesh and bone palace,
forces me to audience with her clout.
I bow to multiplicity,
frilled and spiked globes,
her fever scepter laid on my head.

I stay in the cabin, disheartened, dizzy
and yearn for mountain paths
I see from my porch. The delicious
cold lakes. But she has missives for me,
unscrolling through blunt fatigue,
cough and breathlessness.

> *Every step*
> *you take is home.*
> *No need*
> *for mountain paths.*
> *Sleep is sacred.*
> *Fever a key out of my realm*
> *if you're lucky.*
> *For now your body*
> *is mine, a bloom*
> *of millions that are not you.*
> *That are. You*
> *are the mountain.*

II

As I sit dazed and wait
for a healing muse on the porch
under pine light and shadow,
my sketchbook open to unfinished
watercolors of insects—bumblebee,
buckeye, water strider, blue darner,

all creatures I've noticed
these past malaise days,
a brown fleck drifts to the page.
At first I think—a dry stem
exclamation-point-size, but no.
There's a head and six legs.

Its thread-thin mouthpart drops
and probes the page tasting the art.
Or is it predaceous on other insects,
mistaking image for real? Transfixed,
I see I've been waiting for her,
to paint mystery this small.

She's filament thin, dream-sheer
yet her gracile girder legs
superbly buttress
her slightest motion.
She's not afraid though I shift
and my shade falls across her.

I have no brush this narrow
to render antennae, two dot eyes
and comma wings. Her legs
hair-strands with tiny knobbed joints.
She strides across the page
and tastes the watercolor again.

Nearby damp paint pans gleam
in the sun, lakes by her measure.
No frail visitation, she leaves me at last
with a solid love in my belly for things
I don't understand, all things equal, a tree,
a brush, a stilt bug with a taste for art.

III

Finally the Queen leaves me humbled,
dazed by her indifferent glories
as she rolls on seeking other subjects.
I'm glad to be alive.
To be well enough, though she
grants me a cloak of fatigue.

Even lightning claps on the granite ridge
above the lake that jolt me
on my first walk after being laid low
can't compare to her wild dominion.
The Queen simply wants to live

and live even as she dies,
leaving questions to my jangled mind,
while my flora and fauna
don't worry over things
but settle at home once more
in the dark forests of my body.

Portrait of the Poet as a Young Woman Holding a Hawk

I'm held by the sun-gold eye, wings broad as the mountains
behind us, pungent with sweet sage, tangy sumac, granite,

mineral bones of earth come to surface, crumble and dust,
the six directions lodged within us this moment together.

No one can part our wings one from the other, as I hold him
wing wide in beauty, flight feathers pointing to larger passage.

Hawk who came to us one afternoon, leather jesses dangling
from his feet on the branch above us, then stayed the night.

What could we do but feed the sacred life, though
I was only beginning to know what that could mean.

He stayed for days in our garden until my father cut the jesses,
whatever loyalty he once knew, to release him to the wild.

So many cut loose. The hawk freed. My father disappeared.
I moved away. My mother left my sister. Each to our own

wilderness. Now years later I study the photograph found
in an old manila envelope, new wilds ahead in the vastness

of memory. Young woman in a ponytail, perch hand & arm
gloved in thick leather, hawk bent at the prospect of flight.

I consider what sacred life I must feed. Before I bend to pain
or death I want to offer praise, thanks for that rare visitation,

raptor rising to the oak, then away until I see him no more.
For his slight weight on my forearm. For the warm infant scent

of his feathers (do hawks watch over newborns?).
Hasn't he always been with me? For far vision and close

sight that bring me into balance with spirit. For his shrill call
that enters me keening, yet lifts me to praise. May I rise

like the red-tailed hawk, shed a flight feather for those
left behind, to play with the wind, to mark what can't be seen.

Hot Winds, Wildfire, Ochre Leaves

Asakusa Rice Fields

—Detail from *One Hundred Famous Views of Edo*

Beyond the screen
dark grains scatter

across the sky
no—a flock of birds

call to one another,
unaware of Hiroshige,

the cat, you or me.
So in our small lives

we sing, not knowing
how many listen.

Deer

—for my students

There was something I wanted to say
that can't be contained in a syllabus
or outlined on the chalkboard
(though I love the feel of a smooth
new piece of chalk, its crisp mark).
            Like those two deer in the high Sierras
I saw off trail two weeks ago or didn't see
until I could almost touch them.
Their pattern leapt from shadows,
they were that still
joined with granite, red fir,
the secret creek beneath wildflowers.
The deep eyes, vigilant
far beyond anything human,
the newly furred antlers motionless
as forest in the dead heat of afternoon,
the bodies still as compressed springs.
I simply stopped and said, *Ah,*
and they didn't move until
the fawn stepped toward me, curious.
Sometimes the world comes
forward to meet us.
Grace may lie in a small observance.
Even a word or idea like those deer
has been waiting for you a long time.
Let silence be your guide then,
be open to the wild gift
you each carry within.

The Creek Scent of Home

If traces of salmon rise to
the uppermost branches of spruce,
after bear lap their salty orange roe
and wolves drag the spent curves
of their lives flashing into the woods,

might we not also rise from
the lost days scattered behind us,
after the broken feasts,
after hurtling ourselves again and again
into weightless blinding light?

The Weight of a Dragonfly

Makes all the difference
in the long sweep of a bent cattail leaf,
its pointed yellow tip mysteriously
drifting on the water, up and down
in slow motion, a dancer's arc.
The other elegant leaves barely quiver.
It has a life of its own
toward the end of its soggy life,
all the way down to the root,
beginning to rot and let go.
Yet this last repetitive motion
as it dips when the dragonfly lands,
springs back after the red darner snaps
into flight is the most constant act
of bowing to the dragonfly, to the whole
world in thanks for its quiet life
in the pond as a single leaf
trailing its finger across the water.
No more, no less than my own slim life
only more graceful, less full of doubt.
If the dragonfly should land on me,
I'd want to be easy enough in my silence,
to retell its gesture of love.

The Sigh in the Moon

the pale in the smile
breath in the night
heart upside down

sky in the hands
heat in the stars
solace in silence

together we lean
into fall
hold one another

as dark comes again
old friend, storyteller
to harvest our dreams

A Pause in Our Conversation

I glance up to find
the dusk moon. Sea-cliffs
bleed russet. A moon
half-full of bone-light,
half-full of marrow-dark, drifts
in fleshy cerise clouds, sky become
the inner chamber of an immense body.

Then high above us
in just that moment hundreds of birds,
pelicans in soft V-formation
perfect as a tender line of sutures,
lean and curl and V again across
the moon, mending all wounds with beauty
all chaos with their silent letter of flight.

Wind

My Kansan grandma once said,
I love to walk in the wind!
those big open plains,
grasses combed clean
of their secrets.

For me it's always the desert,
Santa Anas gusting from Great Basin
all wild bluster and sagebrush tang,
hungry winds bearing down
on the coast and kicking up the sea.

Wind of quick twitchy thoughts,
chafing heart.
Wind of chalk-red despair, dark sparks
and fire in the hills.
Death is always coming. So is life.

Wind of broken sleep, rough gullies where
bones bleach down to pure discipline.
Wind of no disputes, no lies.
Wind of small yellow flowers
like butter curls on a vast arid plate.

Limb-breaker, dream-stealer wind,
big mind of god clears our thoughts
kind of wind,
nothing left but an empty stunned
hum in my ears.

When I return from a walk
with the old parched voices
risen from waterless places
I find that fear is a feckless thorn
while the world is a hollow drum
thrumming with change.

Don't be afraid of the wind,
my grandma said.

Fire-Followers

Death camas, stinging lupine,
yellow-throated phacelia
all seed in ashes.

The first ones
to emerge
on a fresh burn.

I'd like to follow
such fierce design, awaken
from scorched earth.

But I'm the seed
that waits out catastrophe
deep underground.

I've made a life of
burrowing, hiding, probing
things in the dark.

Still I look to the fire-followers,
want to cast my hard shell
to the flame.

Break open,
even bloom
on this troubled grey earth.

The Garden

You say you're letting your garden rest.
You've cleared most plants, laid down chips.

Roses still reign in their lovely unfolding
universe and the tomatoes have been stellar.

Sweet, ripe to perfection, lit from within
with that lazy juice that loves to be sauce.

But I like to hear about fallow ground
the becalmed autumn earth that waits, silent.

The way we listen in our gardens for
what wants to come next or maybe

nothing for a while. Like the days before
birth, snug, quiet in the womb until

the last push thrusts you into the light.
How many births do we know in a lifetime?

More than we can comprehend.
But first we must rest, hidden

in a place larger than ourselves,
with all the reverence given to the garden.

In Praise of Chickens

for my grandchildren who persuaded
me to welcome chickens into my garden

Every day I reach into the nest and pull out two warm eggs.
Nothing can compare with a warm egg in hand,
the worldly weight, the fine masonry of the shells
one blue-green, one brown, each housing a sun, a soul,
a sac of the unknown, hope yolked to form
tilting toward a commonplace beauty I can hold
not fully comprehending, yet hold in hand humbly,
turning the marvel round and round as if
it were the center of creation, which it is.
I thank the hens and then on impulse I kiss each egg
with plain love for the ordinary and the sacred.

Telling the Bees

John Chapple, Royal Beekeeper at Buckingham Palace placed black ribbons tied in bows on the hives as he knocked on each one and told them in hushed tones their Mistress had died.

What did the bees say or did they fall
still as quenched embers, all droning done?

Maybe a bee flew to her Balmoral casement
to tap the ancient glass until someone let her in

and she lit on the Queen's lip, carrying one last drop
of honey to Her Majesty's silent tongue.

Or maybe her Soul left her half-open mouth, a worker bee
and flew south to the hives, startling them all

to fresh devotions, tail-wagging dances, flower raptures,
nectar, pollen, egg-laying, wax-building, fanning

the fine hexagonal rooms of her sweet new domain
to keep all the larvae cool and calm, humming

while John Chapple comes after dark
not telling a soul, to sit by the hives and listen.

Long Shadows, Rain, Quickening Roots

Sea Plowed by Dolphins

The cold afternoon gives
rise to undersea eyes, fins,
rolling dorsals, laughing leaps
from salt thoughts after
morsels of air, then deep again,
swimming down to Rome
where my family's fountain,
boy riding a dolphin, spurts
silver from the Tiber, spills
memories of the dauphin, rescued
by a dolphin as I too have been
lifted from drowning in old family
sorrows by the shimmer
of sea revelations.

The finned saints speak
a clicking life I can barely hear
with dry shell ears,
spiral ears for siphoning joy,
inner ears for unfurling
a long wake of sound.
Our boat carves the current west
where dolphins plow
waves in unison, open
the past for a moment before
large swells close on my childhood, leave
only a strand of smooth cabochons,
oval mirrors glistening
on the vast surface of the sea.

Latch

When I was a child, doors were the scariest things in the house.

Unlatched, the door swings open and
the doorframe brackets things in a second:
avocado, squirrel, black dog.

Wallace Stevens would check every door and window

If only I hadn't forgotten to latch the door.
If the dog hadn't shot down the long wooden steps.
If the squirrel hadn't scampered toward the plump avocado.

before he turned out the lights and went to bed.

Or was it because the avid avocado ripened
at the extremity of a limb
and the squirrel coveted the buttery flesh?

Limen, liminal, . . .

Because I forgot to latch the door
and the dog's mind sparked
at the squirrel's tumble?

Some [doors] have minds of their own.

It's the waste that makes me sad.
All the things we allow or
unintentionally kill.

. . . the silent enemy who, once inside, never leaves.

It's dead before I reach the bottom step,
the eye a blind gelatin, golden fur barely still.
My dog stands proudly aside for me to see.

Poetry is all about what comes in.

Maybe I can still do something, I stupidly think
as I touch it, feel in that moment
the heat go, death come on like a freeze.

It's always about keeping things out.

The well-fed dog wags her whole lithe body.
Sick at heart, I move the squirrel outside
the termite-riddled gate beyond her reach.

the door that flashes open

Other squirrels will sniff it
just to make sure, where
I set it beneath the ash tree.

flapping open and closed

I pet my dog, pick up the heavy
avocado, still good for a salad, and walk up
the stairs into the house. Latch the backdoor.

Note: Italicized quotes are taken from an interview with Robert Kelly by Celia Bland

All Winter Long

Chainsaws rev against the trees in our city,
amputate mornings and afternoons,
hum like giant termites gnawing god. A neighbor
asks to have his trees felled rather than see them maimed.

I counter every grief with my night-grinding
rosary of teeth, fierce jaws working each prayer bead
in outrage, blessed be the pungent eucalyptus
breathing through sleek leaves in the fog,

blessed be the palms, tongues of wind, roots of water,
the pepper tree at dusk, its spicy whiff of Brazil,
the mock orange, balm for melancholy,
stone pines that now bleed sap.

I counter grief with prayer though I want
to stop those wielding ordinance and ignorance.
The mind can be a terrible chainsaw,
even when it idles between cuts.

The tree-fellers start at the crown, slice off hunks
then finally poison the stump. Blessed be all the ghost trees.
I also try to pray for my neighbors, may the large view
they've gained, enlarge the view within. I try.

November Garden

We enter muffled against
the cold through Japanese gates
drenched with fog.
Wood smells like regret.
Water drips into the stone bowl,
silence leaking resolve.
Last night I spoke too much
and you answered little.
Today we hold gloved hands
under bare twisted wisteria.
A young couple asks us
to take their picture
beside the crooked stream.
Crooked to fool the demons,
you remind me,
for they love straight lines.
Then we ask the young woman
to take ours too,
a middle-aged couple
under the weeping cedars.

Somewhere a gardener's
rapid snip and spring-assist squeak
of pine bud shears, plucks
the dead and needless
away from the limbs,
even as other unseen clippers
cut and snap open repeatedly
in the rice paper fog.
Sumi sound.
Something returns when
something is taken away.
We walk and listen.
Less is more
my old art teacher often

recited, his wispy
white beard like that
of the tiny clay monk
set in the moss of pine roots.
Some things are gone, some
sleep, others are getting ready.

A maple holds on
to one last rumpled leaf.
Camellia buds point
at the cloud-flocked sun.
Brown iris spears
sheared down to inches
don't even stir under
wet leaf quilts.
We are so cold we laugh
as we shelter
in the heated bathroom
to warm ourselves.
When we leave the garden
we pass out into the world
lighter, chastened by winter,
warmed by each other.
Just up the hill a folding saw
snaps open, then cuts on the pull
as it lops a large limb
that falls into the canyon.

Draw Near

After years of drought
and now days of rain,
she lies in her morning
bed and dreams her hands
trace the flannel-soft bark
of the damp redwood tree listening
on the other side of the wall.

Does it sense her sly touch
that whispers toward sap stirring
around the old heartwood?
To be this still, drawing water.
These green limbs flung
toward alizarin dawn.
To be this sweet ancient surge.

She feels it lean there
toward her house, groaning
with northerly wind, humming
with slow saturant joy as pools
of recent reveille rain seep through
duff into a mat of roots.

Draw near, the tree says,
lift toward light.
Swell like breath rising
your blood mind a capillary
motion, your body a lilt and
rustle, your heat a pungent steam.

When you arch your
winged bone spine
to bear us up even further,
I'll lift you to the needle leaf tips
of my crown that brush
the aqueous blue eyes of heaven.

What a Woman Sees From the Back Door

A man prunes trees
and three children play.

I don't know
what kind of trees

but guess—plum, peach,
persimmon.

The season
winter,

best time
for pruning.

The children
her own heart's joy.

I don't know
the woman

who passed
this winter

just after
the light returned.

But when I hear
the words spoken

of her most complete
moment

another afternoon
comes to me.

The amber slant
of December light

a black dog
jubilant with smells

along the pine-
needled path

my daughter
and husband

walking with me
on the ridge

salt air of the
unseen sea close by.

The ordinary life,
passing.

End of February

Creek-side dusk—we stand still for small
brown birds like fleeting doubts that come and go,

point us to gifts as they glean willow twigs
for insects, chatter, tend pendant nests communally

woven of lichen, webs, feathers, catkins,
memories flecked with light and shadow,

baskets of tiny eggs, yolk-yellow suns
couched in the dark. Yet even in wonder

we feel alone in the troubled world. They lisp tseet-
tseet, as if to scold our grey qualms.

The birds, *psaltriparus minimus*—Latin
for tiny lute-player, pluck the air all around,

plectrums of passing moment and urge. They twine
the last bits of day into nests and sing us

through the lambent willows as night descends,
holy earth spins, and the tiny makers of worlds fall silent.

Steady

At the observatory I find myself
yearning for storm. Even my grandchild,
hand pressed to the plasma dome, noble gases,
electrode at center, yearns fiercely.
Green electricity springs to her touch.
Lightning yearns for us too,
pulses down and up, back and
forth in an instant like thoughts flashing
through me, cranium gone to sky
where all that matters is this instant & this &
all weather wants equilibrium
even if change remains constant.

Love crackles under my fingertips
for the child's staticky hair, the ka-boom of the
heart's contraction, for dragonfly wings,
cicadas in summer's dead heat,
long winds buzzing the lines.
Even ancient oceans sparked life.
My grandchild drops her hand from
the dome as love pops
from her fingertips charged
with that old magnetism toward mine.
Shocked, we laugh and recoil,
then clasp hands again, steady for now.

A/wake

> *Like us, vultures rely on death for sustenance. . .*
> *On the ground, a group of vultures is called a committee.*
> *In flight, they're a kettle.*
> *When feeding, a wake.*

I

I saw the committee once
as I walked by butcher stalls
in Mérida after a bullfight
black-cloaked crinkled
grey-headed crones hunched
together on the wall
wise *xopilotes* in patient
deliberation, waiting
to eat death,
to sing grunt-songs
and hiss-songs, to
purify the world.

II

In old age I pray
for their wild fortitude,
willingness to dip
into mystery, be fed.
I pray for the grace
to welcome them
as once I watched in awe
the kettle of wings
circling the thermals
black soaring
calligraphy
penned against blue fate.

III

When I'm gone
I pray my loved ones
find stories to feed on
at my wake, when
enshrouded by vast black
wings I'm borne
across the edge
of this life into another,
or simply across
as they break me
down into
the whole.

About the Author

Regina O'Melveny is an artist and writer whose work has been published in literary magazines such as *The Bellingham Review, The Sun, West Marin Review,* and *Barrow Street*. Her poem, *Fireflies,* won the Conflux Press Nature Poetry Award, released as an artist's book designed by Tania Baban. She has published three chapbooks: *Secret, New* and *other gods* which won a prize from the Munster International Literary Centre in Ireland. Full-length poetry books include *Blue Wolves,* winner of the Bright Hill Press award, and *The Shape of Emptiness* from Sheila-Na-Gig Editions. Her novel, *The Book of Madness and Cures*, published by LiĮ le, Brown and Company, was listed as one of the six best historical novels of the year by NPR when it was released. Her recent second novel, *The Sea-Cure,* is from Running Wild Press. She tends a coastal sage scrub garden for pollinators in Rancho Palos Verdes, California.

S
Sheila-Na-Gig Editions

www.ingramcontent.com/pod-product-compliance
Ingram Content Group UK Ltd.
Pitfield, Milton Keynes, MK11 3LW, UK
UKHW042012190726
13854UKWH00005B/2259

9 781962 405904